ONE
WAY
TO
LISTEN

POEMS

ASA DRAKE

GOLD LINE PRESS

Book design: Sandra Rosales
Published: Gold Line Press
http://goldlinepress.com
Gold Line titles are distributed by Small Press Distributions
This title is also available for purchase directly from the publisher
www.spdbooks.org: 800.869.7553

Library of Congress Cataloging-in-Publication Data
One Way to Listen
Library of Congress Control Number 2022947906
Drake, Asa
ISBN: 978-1-938900-45-7

"*Those of us in the first American generations have had to figure out how the invisible world the emigrants built around our childhoods fits in solid America.*"

—*Maxine Hong Kingston,* The Woman Warrior

Contents

One Way to Listen

I cut branches from the money tree, surely
unlucky. A jackal's head—no matter
what body we find it on—is a sign of death.
But then the good news, announcements,
store credit. And still, a jackal's head,
if I move carelessly, will enter my kitchen.
I can't recognize my ghosts today. This one
has an 80s windbreaker and short curls,
and my mother asks if I'm sure she's not
a woman in white instead of a white woman.
She's a white woman looking at my wedding
photos, I tell my mother. *But what*
does she feel like, my mother presses. I
don't know every woman who made me.

When the Moon is Your Mother's Lost Comb

Woman who puts up her hair comb holds up
the sky. There is the legend and probably a lie.

My mother felt tired with her jewelry on.
Between me and the forty days to heaven

is the fact that I don't have my receipt.
Today I photograph myself, unmarried.

I pull a silver tine off the back of the moon,
so there's no return policy left for the moon.

What a wall over me made of silk
which was once money itself. If you

are unhappy, come down Moon. Let me go
to work at the coif with you. Turn yourself in

to the woman who spends all her money
at midnight. Which is to say money is in

your possession. It is midnight.
Moon, let me borrow your teeth.

Moon, won't you let down your yes.

Letter to My Younger Self

In this country, the shy don't eat one orange.
If you leave home, you eat and speak like the dead.
This morning, I took both fruits from the municipal
tree but I couldn't take salt from the table.
Boiling water, before I had put up my hair, I saw
my own dead. He in his translucent undershirt, leaning
into the I-don't-know-what for his breakfast, his face
smooth and dark like a real thing. The body I had dressed
blue removed his shirting. The ocean that had swallowed
him rendered salt on my table. We're looking at the orange
blossoms together. If they're no use to him, then they're
blooming for me. Even in summer I fear sharing. I won't
say aloud the short list of my homecomings. I don't
name the hours I take to put up my hair, but they are mine.

Disagreeable Aspects of Hyphenation

Driving through the South wearing my mother's clothes vs. someone who visits like they don't know how to approach a wasp nest.

A co-worker explains there's nothing special about the food I grew up with. I had invited her into my home. I had picked fruit from my own yard, food I'd grown because it was impossible to buy. She had packed a to-go plate for her husband. That's when she told me, leaving, *There's nothing special about the food you grew up with.*

I forget to protect my teeth, and now I find craze lines in the enamel.

The webinar trainer asks that I practice. *What are you going to say?* It is so easy to know how another will root out my provenance. Less to understand what I want from this conversation I don't want.

I don't know.

To protect my teeth, I put my tongue between the bite. I don't think the dead are waiting for us to do anything in particular. It's been 24 years and I still carry a nest of small animals. This year's is the first that survives. Something I've touched that lives, so this is the least of my sins.

Remember, America is only one possibility.

Online, the silk advertises I can sleep anywhere and shows me bodies asleep in the desert. Here the snakes don't bite. They wrap around me under a silk gown and keep their mouths closed. Keeping our mouths closed keeps us warm. We're in this together. Dreaming a man—not the lover— gets too close, so close we all open our mouths.

Who's happier than Medusa? I think I hear my lover, but I've misheard him. He was cutting her up. Who's halved more than Medusa?

I can't say. There are a million things you can halve in the world. A million you can't.

Lola Tells Me to Put Apple Blossoms into Her Hair

I pay for them in lack of apples. She doesn't know
anything about how to protect her own life, only her fruit
and flowers. All the time I have been living, Lola's owned
our houses and the houses she didn't own, she owned
until she started to own something else. Every heirloom
I could ask for, Lola fed me. For decades, she'd saved
her milk. I was close to something delicious, but I was
unlucky. Two years, I misspelled my lola's name
on her tax returns. Now her lender doesn't recognize her.
She tells me in the first house the termite lost its teeth,
sweet on the load bearing beam. *I've lost my teeth*,
I tell her, *wish that on everyone who does you wrong.*

I Worry My Mother Will Die and I Will Know Nothing

Sometimes, history is too beautiful to be believed.
Until dinnertime, my grandmother sold gardenias

wrapped in banana leaves. Then she found
better ways to earn a living. Years later, at an

American restaurant, I'm mistaken for a waitress
wearing all my silk. An accident I knew in my body

like the pride I felt when my adult mother said
I have narrow feet. Mother warns me, *Nothing will*

change. I'm alive and you don't know anything.
It was winter when my mother spoke, apples

rolling in the backseat, the fragrance shifting off-
site under the great deterrent of rain. It's still winter,

with a brown leaf staining my work
slacks. I smell the tea olives working up

spring (or the luxury of that kind of thinking
in January) when I explain to another

that my lunch wasn't useful. All my life,
I've wanted to lay with my stomach to the grass.

I've wanted to eat from community gardens.
I wrote a lie I'll admit now. I didn't eat

the municipal fruit. I bought the Cosmic Crisp
over the Honeycrisp for a dollar surcharge because

I wanted extra shelf life. The last day of the week, I split
the apple to decide if it's for sharing or eating whole.

It's a luxury to have your hunger. I'm sure I don't need to
go back, but can we go back to the restaurant? I am
   laughing

with the woman at the table next to mine about the
   woman
who would have me serve while I celebrate. She was
   going

to eat one dish, and I've ordered five. You know
I'll still leave hungry because I don't tell you

what I eat. See the phoenix with its mouth and feet
   grasping
for two servings? I am where I come from.

In the Tradition of Women Who've Blessed Me to Transfer Their Virtues

I give you what I don't have.
Strawberries in the mouths

of birds. Unopened pomegranate
blossoms devoured by ants. Fruit dropped

from unpollinated vines, all varieties.
Tell me the last time a flower wasn't

the shortcut to desire. One year
in the middle of my life

I asked, *how full do I want to be.*
Like hunger in the years before,

I asked fullness to be endless.
Every noise, I gave cause to.

An excuse to find comfort
in the sounds of eating,

the small soul cutting a summer
lawn. I hear the thrum and wait

in my hothouse for dinner
to line up petal to petal.

Plant fruit I've germinated
in my own mouth. Let

the animals in. I mean
to say I'm in love

with that small mouth.
But I can't call love out

without telling the difference
between one mouth in the grass

and another. Permission is a fruit
I've cut from the tree, meaning

I've taken human sacrifice.
When I say *be careful*

I want to use your hands
in place of my hands.

When I feed the animals
the rabbit stands up

so straight she falls over.
That is the part I want

you to know. We are
that kind of animal.

American Crow Delivers a Message to My Younger Self

Because I want you to know I am happy sometimes, eating blueberries through the confederate park, which is the only park. I came home knowing who my neighbors would be.

When a man approaches me out of the Antietam names, unhappy with my arrangement low in the grasses. Or how I have removed my hat. (Such a large hat!) Or maybe he's seen how I continue my life in unthinkable ways, a person who can forget and be happy. You never thought the South could love me, but a dozen crows set into the pecan grove. The loudest crows I've ever heard, and the man has something to say that I will not hear. I hear only crows. I make them my own breath, but a human breath is less than a dozen crows. A dozen crows is a man walking away from me, so I continue to lunch in a park—I could love this place if I didn't know the reason for it. I am telling you about crows like they work for me because I have let them mean something. It would be enough for no one to approach a small grouping of trees without me knowing, this one parcel, which is whole, and broken down by nothing.

I'm Interested in How Animals Teach Us Pleasure

Sometimes the thing that may destroy
your home sings. I love that song too.

Room for uncertainty.

*Make room in yourself for the longest sentence
you have yet to say.* That was my only singing lesson.

For safety, I abandoned any clothes preoccupied with
   language, even
a dry rotted rice sack

with the word *sweet*. Even hair clips inscribed
with clarity: *don't* and *touch*.

Today, I looked for the smallest iteration of myself.

I am thinking of ordering plums from California
because at this moment they are on the tree

and at 11 a.m. they will not. I am in love
with this kind of transparency.

Room for uncertainty.

A friend reads fortunes in my hair when my lover won't, love
refracted between us to make everyone in the room more
   beautiful.

And still, someone enters to ask if I wasn't born lucky.
I keep a whole rabbit to help me survive. Oh, it eats

and eats at what I was born with. Beloved, if I titled this poem
My Mother's America, would it contain her mother? How long

before you know the urgency of this sentence is lost?

A Co-worker Asks if I'm Superstitious

No, but there's only so much salt water anyone can swallow.

Letter to My Younger Self

When I see men digging clay beside the confederate
monument, I want to know if this is where we bury
unspecific history. Make it look easy.

Lately, I worry. Today I was told
most mixed-race women die in fiction, which implies
that the living version of myself is difficult

for others to imagine. Today a crossing light,
swallowed by the rainy season, joined the number
of things I've touched that fall into sinkholes. All space

I didn't know I was risking. I worry a great deal
about the unimportant ways you busy your hands.
Get thee to a dry cleaner, my love.

Let someone else play human. The woman behind me
can't stand to look. *Who could do that every day*, she says,
like each night I boil moths myself and spin silk.

When A Man Sleeps with My Effigy

Another insists my best protection is property
survey flags, annexed easements, an exterior
not given over to motion. In the aisles
of the early 2000s, I would not have anticipated
my house dress going viral, thus selling out,
thus becoming so ubiquitous to dress an effigy.
A man shows me his purchase and explains
he has named it after me. Do I say this is not my body?
If that is not enough, I go inside, house myself
in accumulation so precious as to have survived
eight apartments. Wrap my actual body in knife pleats
set each week by a lover's hand. Shimmy
into inherited brocade, smocked stiff as the grave.
This is not to say an effigy cannot be made,
but what is a body rendered without detail,
and I am a woman who hates to be naked.

T. and I Compare the Dreamscape

On his side of the border, we spend the night in a waiting room reading subtitles.

On my side, he cuts my bangs perfectly with garden secateurs.

I dead-headed roses to my own height in the new p.m. of daylight savings. Easy-care varieties of difficult flowers, like a crossbreed of two roses, which is still a hybrid, though both parents are roses. Thus I believe there is some shameful memory here.

Overnight, a man travels through multiple counties professing desire. Being public-facing, I can't help but think of how often I offer assistance and am asked to gratify.

The news hesitates to mention hate after the gunman's confession. They recount a man *lashing out* as police insist on his insistence that *he had not targeted the victims, six of whom were of Asian descent, because of their race.*

I spend an hour getting dressed in clothing appropriate for a grief no one will recognize. All my gestures reduced to desire.

And still, I have time to tell my lover that the dreamscapes we recount are connected.

When the moon isn't anything but two leaves unfolding for a fortnight, what have you got on you in that moment of exaltation?

Substitute desire now in each previous recitation.

Desire, meaning I hear the moon rattle, tooth loose from the gun. I will never interpret it otherwise.

I Don't Know How to Talk About Racism, so I Call My Mother About the Indispensable Pleasure of Material Things

It is night in my house. I imagine one room
safer than the rest. Other people really do exist,

and this is not a comfort. Tonight I have
no terrible news. This week my lover

works late, so the windows overwhelm
their steel frames, opening. This week I look

like my mother in the daytime, drawstring shorts,
red scrunchie, planting lemongrass and ginger

borders, bromeliads in the trees. I hear a lot
of people move south these days for that. Mom

down in Coral Gables instagramming her vandas
because an orchid isn't an orchid, it's specific.

Look down on the species. Tell which leaves
signify expense, and none will last my life.

No need, but the woman tonight, to file her SSN,
she lived through her ages twice. I hear even

the SSN isn't eternal, so tonight, the woman
is anyone I love too much to bring attention to.

She says the fear keeping me up is my dream
where the lotus paste vanishes, the animals

are small but endless, and I am looking for
the one I own. I don't want to go further.

She's just closed on her house. Neither of us know
if the things we buy will last our lives. I want to know

dreams without worry. I ask my lover what he dreams.
He dreams our windows are in the Midwest. They are broken.

In the dream, he can't find our insurance. Like all
monthly recurrences, I keep the insurance to myself.

Dreamscape Dressed in My Younger Self

First, you have a dress of gold, but
you can't wear it. The gold dress cannot
be washed or dry cleaned. Hell, the tag
says no spot cleaning. So you have a dress
of gold, just in case. Then a field of red sorrel
in rows like someone loves it. Then a pine
forest with a dogwood floor. Next the Perseids
behind sheet lightning. Next-year fruit
from your own cuttings. Slice me fruit
from the year I have yet to grow. I couldn't slice
a pomegranate with less than six cuts.
Once you learn, there's only one way to prepare
the pip-star in each soft pear. I have seen illustrations,
and I have been scolded by so many women
for making indefensible halves at their pie table. Now,
remember that dress we're saving. You try it on.

Notes

The epigraph comes from Maxine Hong Kingston's *The Woman Warrior: Memoirs of a Girlhood Among Ghosts* (Knopf, 1976).

"Disagreeable Aspects of Hyphenation" ends with an altered quotation from *Star Trek*, season one, episode two.

"T. and I Compare the Dreamscape" includes a quotation from *The New York Times*' March 17, 2021 article "8 People Killed in Atlanta-Area Massage Parlor Shootings" and a reference to cotton leaves grown on the moon based on a report from *Popular Science* October 14, 2019.

In "I'm Interested in How Animals Teach Us Pleasure," the plums are from Penryn Orchard, the hair clips are from Chunks.

"Letter to my Younger Self" references "Letter Four" in Paisley Rekdal's *Appropriate: A Provocation*.

Acknowledgments

Thank you to the editors of the following journals, in which earlier versions of these poems appeared:

The Adroit Journal, "I Worry my Mother Will Die and I Will Know Nothing," August 2020

The Margins, "When the Moon is Your Mother's Lost Comb" and "Letter to my Younger Self," September 2018

Copper Nickel, "I'm Interested in How Animals Teach Us Pleasure," Fall 2022

The Georgia Review, "Disagreeable Aspects of Hyphenation" and "T. and I Compare the Dreamscape," Spring 2022

Paris Review Daily, "This Is One Way to Listen," May 2020

Poetry Northwest, "Letter to my Younger Self," April 2022

The Slowdown, "I Worry my Mother Will Die and I Will Know Nothing," October 2021

Southern Humanities Review, "Dreamscape Dressed in my

Younger Self" and "American Crow Delivers a Message to my Younger Self," March 2021

Superstition Review, "Lola Tells Me to Put Apple Blossoms into Her Hair," May 2019

Tupelo Quarterly, "In the Tradition of Women Who've Blessed Me to Transfer Their Virtues," November 2019

Asa Drake is a Filipina American writer and poet in Central Florida. She is the recipient of fellowships and awards from the 92Y Discovery Poetry Contest, Tin House and Idyllwild Arts. Her poems can be found in *The American Poetry Review, Copper Nickel, The Georgia Review* and *Poetry Northwest.*